General Power of Attorney Kit

A Special Request

Your brief Amazon review could really help us!

This link will take you to the Amazon.com review page for this book.

Estate-bee.com/review7

Estate Bee

By EstateBee Publishing

Bibliographic Data

- International Standard Book Number (ISBN): 978-1-913889-04-3
- Printed in the United States of America
- First Edition: December 2010
- Second Edition: January 2014
- Third Edition: July 2020

Published By: EstateBee Limited
23 Lynn Road
London SW12
United Kingdom

Printed and Distributed By: Kindle Direct Publishing, an Amazon Company

For more information, e-mail books@estate-bee.com.

Copyright

Trademarks

All terms mentioned in this kit that are known to be trademarks or service marks have been appropriately capitalized. Use of a term in this kit should not be regarded as affecting the validity of any trademark or service mark.

Warning and Disclaimer

Although precautions have been taken in preparing this kit, neither the publisher nor the author assumes any responsibility for errors or omissions. No warranty of fitness is implied and all implied warranties are excluded to the fullest extent permitted by law. The information is provided on an "as is" basis. Neither the author nor the publisher shall be liable or responsible to any person or entity for any loss or damages (whether arising by negligence or otherwise) arising from the use of or reliance on the information contained in this kit or from the use of any forms or documents accompanying it.

Important Note

This kit is meant as a general guide to preparing your own general power of attorney. While effort has been made to make this kit as accurate as possible, laws and their interpretation are constantly changing. As such, you are advised to update this information with your own research and/or counsel and to consult with your personal legal, financial and/or medical advisors before acting on any information contained in this kit.

The purpose of this kit is to educate and entertain. It is not meant to provide legal, financial or medical advice or to create any attorney-client or other advisory relationship. The authors and publisher shall have neither liability (whether in negligence or otherwise) nor responsibility to any person or entity with respect to any loss or damage caused or alleged to be caused directly or indirectly by the information contained in this kit or the use of that information.

About EstateBee

EstateBee, the international self-help legal publisher, was founded in 2000 by lawyers from one of the most prestigious international law firms in the World.

Our aim was simple - to provide access to quality legal information and products at an affordable price.

Our will writing software was first published in that year and, following its adaptation to cater for the legal systems of various countries worldwide, quickly drew in excess of 40,000 visitors per month to our website. From this humble start, EstateBee has quickly grown to become a leading international estate planning and asset protection self-help publisher with legal titles in the United States, Canada, the United Kingdom, Australia and Ireland.

Our publications provide customers with the confidence and knowledge to help them deal with everyday estate planning issues such as the preparation of a last will and testament, a living trust, a power of attorney, administering an estate and much more.

By providing customers with much needed information and forms, we enable them to place themselves in a position where they can protect both themselves and their families through the use of easy to read legal documents and forward planning techniques.
The Future....

We are always seeking to expand and improve the products and services we offer. However, to do this, we need to hear from interested authors and to receive feedback from our customers.

If something isn't clear to you in one of our publications, please let us know and we'll try to make it clearer in the next edition. If you can't find the answer you want and have a suggestion for an addition to our range, we'll happily look at that too.

Using Self-Help Kits

Before using a self-help kit, you need to carefully consider the advantages and disadvantages of doing so – particularly where the subject matter is of a legal or tax related nature.

In writing our self-help kits, we try to provide readers with an overview of the laws in a specific area, as well as some sample documents. While this overview is often general in nature, it provides a good starting point for those wishing to carry out a more detailed review of a topic.

However, unlike an attorney advising a client, we cannot cover every conceivable eventuality that might affect our readers. Within the intended scope of this kit, we can only cover the principal areas in a given topic, and even where we cover these areas, we can still only do so to a moderate extent. To do otherwise would result in the writing of a textbook which would be capable of use by legal professionals. This is not what we do.

We try to present useful information and documents that can be used by an average reader with little or no legal knowledge. While our sample documents can be used in the vast majority of cases, everybody's personal circumstances are different. As such, they may not be suitable for everyone. You may have personal circumstances which might impact the effectiveness of these documents or even your desire to use them. The reality is that without engaging an attorney to review your personal circumstances, this risk will always exist. It's for this very reason that you need to consider whether the cost of using a do-it-yourself legal document outweighs the risk that there may be something special about your particular circumstances which might not be taken into account by the sample documents attached to this kit (or indeed any other sample documents).

It goes without saying (we hope) that if you are in any doubt as to whether the documents in this kit are suitable for use in your particular circumstances, you should contact a suitably qualified attorney for advice before using them. Remember the decision to use these documents is yours. We are not advising you in any respect.

In using this kit, you should also consider the fact that this kit has been written with the purpose of providing a general overview of the laws in the United States. As such, it does not attempt to cover all the various procedural nuances and specific requirements that may apply from state to state – although we do point some of these out along the way. Rather, in our kit, we try to provide forms which give a fair example of the type of forms which are commonly used in most states. Nevertheless, it remains possible that your state may have specific requirements which have not been taken into account in our forms.

Another thing that you should remember is that the law changes – thousands of new laws are brought into force every day and, by the same token, thousands are repealed or amended every day. As such, it is possible that while you are reading this kit, the law might well have been changed. We hope it hasn't but the chance does exist. To address this, when we become aware of them, we do send updates to our customers about material changes to the law. We also ensure that our books are reviewed and revised regularly to take account of these changes.

Anyway, assuming that all the above is acceptable to you, let's move on to exploring the topic at hand.........general powers of attorney.

Table of Contents

General Powers of Attorney

What is a Power of Attorney?

A power of attorney (also referred to as a "POA") is a legal document by which you can appoint and authorize another person (usually a trusted friend, family member, colleague or adviser) to act on your behalf and to legally bind you in that respect. While most people fail to see the importance of having a power of attorney, there are many compelling reasons why they should be used.

For example, suppose that:

- you are going to be out of the country for an extended period and need someone trustworthy to manage your business affairs while you're away; or

- you wish to acquire real estate in another state, and you need to authorize a local to sign and lodge documents on your behalf; or

- you want someone to manage your real estate for you; or

- you're getting a little bit older and wish to appoint someone you know and trust to make healthcare decisions on your behalf should the day come when you are unable to do so yourself.

A power of attorney can be used to facilitate your needs in each of these scenarios.

The person giving the power of attorney is usually referred to as the 'donor', 'grantor' or 'principal', while the recipient is called the 'agent', 'attorney-in-fact' or just plain 'attorney' (which doesn't mean they have to be a legal practitioner).

Types of Powers of Attorney

There are several different types of power of attorney that you can make. Each of these serve a different set of needs and requirements. Some of the main types of power of attorney are detailed below.

General Power of Attorney

A 'general power of attorney' is virtually unlimited in scope. It allows your agent to act as your authorized legal representative in relation to the whole cross-section of your legal and financial affairs, until such time as that authorization is terminated. In other words, your agent will have full legal authority to make decisions and take actions on your behalf, as if you were taking them yourself. This could, for example, include signing letters and checks, executing contracts, opening and closing bank accounts, and so on.

While you cannot generally limit the scope of the power conferred under a general power of attorney, there are nonetheless some presumed limits to the agent's authority. For example, your agent is not normally permitted to assume any position or office that you might hold. These offices would include positions as employee, company director, trustee, personal representative, and others. In addition to that, your agent cannot execute a will on your behalf (or amend an existing one), take action concerning your marriage or delegate his or her authorization under your power of attorney to a third party, unless expressly authorized to do so in the power of attorney document. An agent is also prevented from making gifts of your assets, other than small gifts that you yourself might have been expected to make having regard to the size of your estate.

Important Note

It is important to bear in mind that you will remain personally liable for the actions of your agent, so you should grant authorization only to someone you trust implicitly. Where you do grant authorization, you should monitor their actions appropriately. This applies in respect of all types of powers of attorney.

A general power of attorney (unless stated to be durable) automatically comes to an end if you become mentally incapacitated or die. It will also come to an end on any termination date set out in the document itself.

Limited Power of Attorney

A 'limited power of attorney' is like a general power of attorney except that it imposes specific and sometimes substantial limits upon the authorization granted to your agent. This could, for example, be a limit to the scope or duration of the authority granted to your agent.

Often, people granting powers of attorney limit their agent's authority to completing specific transactions or tasks. For example, you may appoint someone as your agent solely for the purpose of having them sign a document on your behalf but only in a format pre-approved by you and attached to the power of attorney document itself. Alternatively, you can appoint your agent for the sole purpose of dealing with a single task or transaction (such as the sale of a piece of real estate to a specified individual at a specified price and on specified terms). These types of limitations remove a substantial part of the risk associated with granting powers of attorney. The good news is that there are no limits on the limitations you can impose on your agent's authority. So, you can be as precise in the authority you grant your agent as you wish.

Like the position with a general power of attorney, you will remain personally liable for the actions of your agent.

The limited power of attorney will continue in force until it comes to an end on a date set out in the power of attorney document – assuming there is one. In any event, it will automatically come to an end if you become mentally incapacitated or die.

Healthcare Power of Attorney

One of the most common forms of power of attorney in use today is the 'medical' or 'healthcare' power of attorney.

A healthcare power of attorney allows you to authorize an agent to make healthcare decisions on your behalf if you are incapacitated and unable to make those decisions yourself. The authorization conferred on your agent can cover any form of healthcare decision. Unlike documents such as living wills, the agent's authority under a healthcare power of attorney can apply even where you are not terminally ill or permanently unconscious. So, for example, it could apply if you suffered temporary unconsciousness (if you were in an accident, for instance) or if you were suffering from a mental illness like Alzheimer's disease which affects the decision-making process.

Unlike general and limited powers of attorney, a healthcare power of attorney does not automatically terminate if you become incapacitated. Better still, you can even specify in your healthcare power of attorney document that your agent's authority only comes into effect if your physicians determine that you have become incapacitated or are otherwise unable to make decisions for yourself.

In your healthcare power of attorney document, you can specify guidelines and directions regarding the types of medical treatment you wish to receive during any periods in which you are unable to make healthcare decisions on your own behalf. Other than in the most extreme cases, your agent will be obliged to follow these instructions and direct your physicians to follow them. As an alternative to expressly specifying your wishes, you can also give your agent full discretion to make healthcare decisions on your behalf during any period in which you are unable to. Of course, be mindful who you give such authority to.

Ordinary and Durable Powers of Attorney

In addition to the three types of powers of attorney that we have just described, powers of attorney can also be categorized as either being 'ordinary' or 'durable'.

Ordinary powers of attorney are only valid for as long as you can make decisions on your own behalf. If you die, or become mentally incapacitated, your power of attorney immediately ceases to have effect and your agent's authority immediately comes to an end. If this happens, your family and business partners could be left in a situation where they are powerless to legally deal with your affairs without seeking court intervention. Some examples of typical problems include the inability to transfer real estate held in joint names, deal with bank accounts that require dual signatories, and the execution of legal documents generally.

Durable powers of attorney, on the other hand, remain valid even if you become mentally incapacitated. In fact, under many durable powers of attorney, your agent's authority to act only becomes effective if you become incapacitated. By giving a trusted family member, friend, or adviser authority to legally make decisions on your behalf while incapacitated, you can ensure that your family's interests and business interests are protected. Of course, like all powers of attorney, durable powers of attorney will come to an end if you die.

In a durable power of attorney that only becomes effective if you become incapacitated, it is usual to see a clause which provides that a doctor must personally examine you and determine that you are incapacitated and unable to handle your financial affairs before your agent's authority will come into effect. It is that determination that then acts as the trigger for your agent's authority to commence.

To be recognized as durable, your power of attorney must contain a clear and unambiguous statement to the effect that it is intended to be 'durable'. It is also helpful to include an express statement to the effect that 'this power of attorney shall not be affected by my subsequent incapacity' or that 'this power of attorney shall become effective upon my incapacity'. Statements of this type help make it clear that your power of attorney was intended to be durable and to be valid even if or after you became incapacitated.

Springing Powers of Attorney

A 'springing' power of attorney is one that becomes effective at a future time or on the occurrence of a future event. That event could include your incapacity or might be something as simple as the date upon which you complete the purchase of a piece of real estate, open a bank account, or otherwise. Springing powers of attorney can be general or limited, as well as ordinary or durable. They can even be healthcare powers of attorney.

Mutual Powers of Attorney

Mutual powers of attorney are usually made between a husband and wife, and occasionally between the members of smaller businesses or professional firms. They serve as indicators of the mutual trust, confidence, and reliance that the parties enjoy within their relationship.

Under these powers of attorney, each spouse or partner will appoint the other (or others) as their agent so as to ensure that their joint plans are implemented in the unfortunate event that one of them is rendered unable to act by illness or injury. For this reason, they are usually durable powers of attorney. As between a husband and wife, they are often durable general powers of attorney (which are unlimited in scope), whereas between business partners they are often durable limited powers of attorney (which, as the name implies, are limited in scope).

Cascading Powers of Attorney

A cascading power of attorney is simply a form of power of attorney which allows for the appointment of alternative or substitute agents. Its purpose is to provide for a backup agent in the event that the first agent named in the power of attorney is unable or unwilling to act, and then provide for further backups to replace the substitute agents if they too decline to act or cannot act for any reason.

Capacity to Make a Power of Attorney

Generally, anyone who has reached the age of majority in their state, who has sufficient mental capacity and who is not an un-discharged bankrupt can make a power of attorney. Even a company or a partnership can make a power of attorney.

Having sufficient mentally capacity to make a power of attorney generally means that you must, at the time of making it, be aware of the nature and extent of your assets and personal circumstances, understand your obligations in relation to your dependents and understand the nature of the power being granted to your agent under your power of attorney.

If you are in any doubt as to whether you have sufficient capacity to make a power of attorney, it is sensible to visit your doctor on the same day as you make your power of attorney and have them complete a certificate acknowledging that, in their medical opinion, you were lucid and mentally aware on the date you make your power of attorney. You could even make the power of attorney in the presence of your doctor for some extra protection. By having a doctor certify your mental capacity in this way, you will help reduce the likelihood that someone would later challenge the validity of your power of attorney on grounds of incapacity.

If, for some reason, you are found by a court or doctors to be incapacitated at a time where you believe you are not, you have the right to petition your local court to request a capacity review hearing for the purpose of affirming or quashing that determination. At any such hearing, you will be entitled to be represented by legal counsel who can present your case for you.

In several states, agents appointed under a power of attorney have a legal duty to notify principals of their right to challenge a determination that they are incapacitated. Agents are also prohibited from trying to prevent principals from contacting a lawyer or asking for a capacity review hearing. However, it is worth remembering that most agents are trusted spouses or family members rather than professionals accustomed to acting as agents under powers of attorney. As such, the likelihood is that the agent will not be aware of his or her obligations in this regard.

The precise requirements for making a power of attorney differ slightly from state to state. If you are in any doubt as to whether you can make a power of attorney due to your personal circumstances, you should obtain the advice of an attorney practicing in your state.

What Does "Incapable" or "Incapacitated" Mean?

You will be deemed to be 'incapable' or 'incapacitated' if you are unable to understand and process information that is relevant to making an informed decision and if you are unable to evaluate the likely consequences of making that decision.

Your power of attorney will usually contain a mechanism for determining whether you are incapacitated or not. In most cases, a power of attorney will provide that one or two doctors or attending physicians will need to agree that you are incapacitated before you are deemed to be incapacitated for the purpose of your power of attorney. If they agree and depending on the type of power of attorney you have made, your agent's powers will come into effect.

Should I Make a Power of Attorney?

The simple answer is "yes". If you have any kind of property or income, it's a good idea to make a durable power of attorney to protect those assets in the event that you become incapacitated and unable to manage your affairs – whether for a short period or a longer term.

The need to make a durable power of attorney is of course greater if you believe that health problems may make it difficult or even impossible for you to manage your affairs in the future. However, even if you have no impending health issues, it's still a good idea to have a durable power of attorney in case you become incapacitated due to an accident or sudden illness. We don't always know what lies around the corner, so it's best to be prepared.

Have you ever considered what would happen if:-

- you were involved in a serious accident which left you in a coma? What would your family do, in both the short and longer term, if they had no power to access your bank accounts, manage your stocks and investments, manage your real estate or take care of your affairs in general?

- you began to have blackouts and act in an out-of-character fashion? You're diagnosed as having a brain tumor and quickly lose the capacity to function normally or make rational decisions. Will your property, financial and other affairs be stuck in limbo?

In both cases, a durable power of attorney would be of great benefit to you and your family. During your incapacity, your agent would be able to manage most practical and financial issues that arise. He or she would be able to access your bank accounts to pay bills and medical expenses, to deposit funds paid to you, to deal with insurance claims and benefits paperwork, and much more.

No doubt many other matters would also need attention such as handling property repairs and lettings, managing investments or even a small business. In most cases, a durable general power of attorney is the best way to take care of all these and other similar tasks.

By preparing a power of attorney now, while you can do so, you can ensure that a person of your choosing is given the task of managing your property, assets and affairs if you become incapacitated. If you don't appoint someone now, then an application may need to be made to court to appoint a conservator to manage your affairs. This would be someone chosen by the court and could be a professional person who you don't know, as opposed to a trusted family member or friend.

What Happens Without a Power of Attorney?

If you become incapacitated without having made a durable power of attorney, it's quite likely that someone will have to apply to the court to be formally appointed to manage your affairs. The persons most likely to do that are members of your immediate family.

In making an application to court, your family will be asking the court to assess your mental capacity and to decide that you are not able to make decisions on your own behalf. In those circumstances, they will also ask the court to appoint someone known as a 'conservator' (which is also commonly referred to as 'guardian of the estate', 'committee', or 'curator'). This will usually be a spouse, adult child, or sibling, and the appointee will be tasked with managing and given the power to manage your affairs while you are incapacitated.

This application to appoint a conservator is often made in public and, in some instances, a notice of the intended application is published in a local newspaper. This can be embarrassing and intrusive. If family members disagree over who is to be appointed as your conservator, the proceedings may become disagreeable and drawn out. This can greatly increase the costs of the application, especially as lawyers will need to be hired.

While the court will often appoint a close family member to act as your conservator, it is not obliged to do so. It can appoint a professional conservator who does not know you, who is not aware of your wishes, and who can legally ignore your family's requests and needs. For this reason alone, conservatorships are best avoided. Of course, you do that by making a durable power of attorney.

When a conservator is appointed, he or she will generally need to:

● post an insurance bond in case he or she decides to steal or misuse your property;

- prepare (or hire a lawyer or accountant to prepare) detailed financial reports relating to your affairs, and periodically file those reports with the court; and

- get court approval before carrying out certain transactions such as selling real estate or making investments.

The cost of doing all of this adds up and ultimately needs to be paid from your estate. Avoiding these types of costs is yet another good reason to consider making a durable power of attorney. When done right, it is a much more flexible and cheaper option compared to a conservatorship.

Do I Really Need a Power of Attorney?

You may think that if you are married, have placed the majority of your possessions in a living trust or hold most of your property as a joint tenant, then you don't need a durable power of attorney. That can certainly be true in some respects; but in each case there is still a strong argument to have a durable power of attorney.

Marriage and Registered Civil Partnerships

If you are married or in a registered civil partnership, your spouse or partner will have a significant degree of authority to deal with property you own together. For example, he or she will be able to access joint bank accounts to pay bills, or sell stocks or shares held in a joint brokerage account. However, there may be certain jointly owned property that they cannot deal with.

In many states, a spouse or civil partner cannot sell jointly owned real estate or automobiles without the written consent of the other. Of course, if the other spouse or partner is incapacitated and cannot give their consent, the sale cannot proceed. This could have important consequences if, for example, assets needed to be sold to pay on-going medical expenses or other important expenses such as a mortgage repayment. If you were the main bread winner in your house, and your income suddenly stopped coming in, assets may need to be sold to pay bills.

If, on the other hand, you held property in your own name only rather than in the joint names of you and your spouse or registered civil partner, he or she will have no legal authority to deal with that property. Unless, of course, they had a durable power of attorney or court order.

Living Trusts

Even if you have taken the time to create a living trust, and transferred most of your assets to the trust, it is still a good idea to have a durable power of attorney.

Under typical living trusts, the person appointed as the 'successor trustee' has the power to distribute the trust assets following the death of the 'grantor'. The grantor is the person who created the trust and transferred the assets into it. He or she normally manages the trust assets until no longer able to do so due to death or incapacity. In the case of incapacity, successor trustees have the power to step in and manage the trust assets on behalf of the trust's beneficiaries.

So, you may think you are covered if most of your assets are held in a living trust. If anything happens you, your successor trustee steps in and manages everything.

Of course, one of the most common problems with living trusts is that grantors often forget to transfer all their assets into the trust, or fail to correctly transfer them in. Suppose you bought investment assets about a month before you suffered a stroke....and you simply never got around to transferring those assets into your living trust. These types of issues happen all the time. Similarly, what if you signed transfer papers to transfer assets into the trust but, unknown to you, they were invalid for some reason. Again, this happens.

For these reasons, it is sensible to have a durable power of attorney just in case things don't' go to plan.

Did You Know

For more information on living trusts, check out our book "Make a Living Trust and Avoid Probate" or our legal kit "Living Trust Kit". Both are available from www.estate-bee.com.

Joint Tenancy

Joint tenancy is a form of joint ownership where each co-owner holds an undivided interest in a piece of property. When one of the co-owners dies, the remaining co-owners automatically inherit the deceased co-owner's share of the property through a right of survivorship.

While matters are relatively straight-forward in the case of death, they can become more complicated where one of the co-owners becomes incapacitated. This is because the other co-owners will often have limited authority to deal with the joint tenancy property without the consent of the incapacitated co-owner.

Real estate provides a good example of this problem. If one co-owner becomes incapacitated, the others have no legal authority to sell or refinance the incapacitated co-owner's share of the property. In that case, they would be stuck holding the real estate on the same financing terms as were in place when the co-owner became incapacitated.

This type of problem could be avoided if the incapacitated co-owner had made a durable power of attorney. That durable power of attorney could authorize an agent to deal with the co-owner's share of joint tenancy property. That could include dealing with bank accounts, re-financings, and sales, as well as insurance and litigation matters. This would then give the remaining co-owners a means by which they could deal with the real estate. They would need the agent's consent of course, but that is something they would have to work on.

The Relationship Between Principal and Agent

As mentioned at the outset, the principal is the person who creates a power of attorney and the agent is the person who the principal authorizes to act on his or her behalf.

Underpinning the relationship between a principal and agent is the requirement that the agent must act with utmost good faith on behalf of, and in the interests of, the principal. It is a relationship built on trust in which the agent is obliged to act with loyalty on behalf of the principal and in accordance with instructions received from the principal. The agent can neither intentionally ignore these instructions nor negligently act in the performance of them. In return for this loyalty, a principal instills confidence and trust in the agent thereby creating a fiduciary relationship of trust and confidence between the parties. It is this relationship of trust and confidence that underpins every action taken or left untaken by the agent.

Unfortunately, human nature being what it is, the principles of trust upon which the fiduciary relationship is built are often honored more on paper than in observance. The reality is that people sometimes succumb to the pressure of other affairs, to a lack of thought about and appreciation of their obligations, and of course to temptation. This risk of breach is the main risk associated with agency relationships particularly because of the agent's ability to legally bind the principal.

Who Can Be an Agent?

While there is no need for your agent to be a lawyer or other professional person, he or she must be an adult capable of making decisions and carrying out specific tasks on your behalf. They should be someone that you trust implicitly and who you feel is up to the task at hand – bearing in mind that the role could be demanding if your affairs are complex.

If you are creating a power of attorney for healthcare, rather than one for finance or property, it may be advisable to weigh the agent's capacity for compassion against their talents as a financial analyst or businessman. Ultimately, the agent's role will help you determine who is best suited to the position.

Your agent cannot be an un-discharged bankrupt and should not be the owner, operator or employee of a nursing home or extended care facility in which you are resident or are likely to be resident. Similarly, your agent cannot be someone who has witnessed your signature on your power of attorney.

Joint or Joint and Independent Agents

When appointing an agent, you will have the freedom to appoint more than one agent to act on your behalf. Doing this gives you an extra degree of comfort that your interests will be protected during any period of incapacity.

If you decide to appoint two or more agents, you will need to give some thought as to whether they should be appointed as 'joint agents' or 'joint and independent agents'.

Joint agents are agents that must act together to make decisions. If you appoint two joint agents, for example, they will need to unanimously agree on a course of action before that action can lawfully be taken on your behalf. When they do act, they will need to take the same action at the same time – whether that is signing a contract or something else on your behalf. If one of the agents is unable or unwilling to act, the other agent then becomes powerless to act. This type of arrangement therefore gives you a degree of protection by removing the possibility that one of your agents will act outside their instructions or in a 'rogue' capacity. Of course, it also carries the risk of inaction if the agents cannot agree on a specific course of action.

Joint and independent agents, on the other hand, can act either together or individually. This means that, even though the agents are both acting on your behalf and in relation to the same matter, they will each be free to take actions on your behalf (and bind you) without the need to consult with or get the agreement of any other agent. This provides a degree of flexibility to each agent to get things done with a little less bureaucracy. It also reduces the possibility of a deadlock between the agents.

It is generally recommended that you avoid appointing joint agents as your power of attorney could become ineffective if your agents were unable to agree on specific courses of action. Instead, it is usually better to appoint a primary agent and then appoint alternate agents who can step in if the primary agent is unable or unwilling to carry out his or her role.

Alternate Agents

While there is no requirement for you to do so, it is usually a good idea to appoint an alternate agent (also known as a substitute agent). If your first named agent is unable or unwilling to act on your behalf, your alternate agent will be able to step in to his or her shoes and carry out the role of agent. In doing so, he or she will have the same level of authority as your original agent had, unless you expressly restrict his or her powers in your power of attorney document.

Often, third parties (such as financial institutions) will require proof that your original agent is unable or unwilling to act under your power of attorney before accepting instructions from your alternate agent. Therefore, if your alternate agent needs to act on your behalf, he or she should request either a signed confirmation from you as principal revoking the authority of the original agent or, if available, a signed confirmation from your original agent confirming in writing his or her refusal or inability to act as agent. These letters of revocation or confirmation can then be presented to the third parties, together with a copy of the original power of attorney, to evidence the authority and power of your alternate agent.

Scope of an Agent's Powers

The scope of your agent's powers will depend on whether the power of attorney you create is general or limited. With general powers of attorney, the scope is generally unlimited. So, your agent is pretty much free to do whatever you could legally do yourself. By contrast, with a limited power of attorney, your agent only has authority to do whatever you have set out in the power of attorney document (assuming you could also legally do those things). That could be the power to carry out a relatively broad scope of things, or it could be limited to carrying out one single specific act. Ultimately, your agent will have as much or as little power as you decide to give him or her.

When considering limiting the scope of your agent's authority, you can limit it in any manner you wish and be as prescriptive as you wish. For example, you could be as prescriptive as to say he or she can only "transfer $100 from my savings account with Bank of America (account number 123456789010) to the HSBC bank account of my wife Rose (account number 473289748327)". Your agent would be able to carry out that transfer on your behalf but nothing else.

Alternatively, you can give your agent a broader, yet still limited, set of powers to do any or all the following things:

(i)   use your assets to discharge the day-to-day expenses of you and your family.

(ii)   purchase, sell, lease, let, maintain, repair, pay taxes on and mortgage real estate and other property.

(iii)   claim and collect social insurance, government, civil, military, and other entitlements.

(iv)   invest money in stocks, bonds, and mutual funds.

(v)   effect transactions with financial institutions.

(vi)   buy, maintain, and sell insurance policies and annuities.

(vii)   file and discharge your tax liabilities.

(viii) operate your small business.

(ix)   claim real estate or other property that you inherit or are otherwise entitled to.

(x)   transfer property into a trust you have created (if the rules of the trust permit).

(xi)   engage someone to represent you in court or to run legal actions on your behalf.

(xii)   manage your affairs generally.

This list is not exhaustive. It merely gives an example of the different scopes of authority you could grant to your agent.

Duties and Responsibilities of an Agent

Your agent has the following primary duties and responsibilities:

- to act in your best interest.

- to keep accurate records of dealings/transactions undertaken on your behalf.

- to act towards you with the utmost good faith and to avoid situations where there is a conflict of interest.

- to keep your property and money separate from their own.

As far as keeping accurate records is concerned, your agent should keep a list or register of:

- all your assets as at the date of his or her appointment or, if later, the date of his or her first transaction on your behalf.

- all assets acquired and disposed of on your behalf, and the date and particulars of each such transaction.

- all receipts and disbursements on your behalf, and the date and particulars of each such transaction.

- all investments bought and sold on your behalf, and the date and particulars of each such transaction.

- all your liabilities as of the date of your agent's appointment, or if later, the date of his or her first transaction on your behalf.

- all liabilities incurred and paid on your behalf, and the date and particulars of each such transaction.

- all compensation taken by the agent and the way it was calculated.

Your agent should keep these records until he or she ceases acting for you and until the date upon which he or she is formally relieved from acting as your agent. These records should be handed over to the agent's successor, or if the power of attorney terminates by reason of your death or incapacity, to your legal personal representative or any successor agent. Of course, if you recover from your incapacity, the records can be given back to you.

Choosing an Agent

As your agent will have a large degree of control and visibility over your assets and affairs, and those of your family, you should choose someone you know and trust thoroughly to act as your agent. After all, your agent will have complete authority to deal with your financial and legal affairs (subject to any limitations specified in your power of attorney) and to bind you as if it was you acting.

In many cases, it makes sense to choose a close family member as they may already have a good degree of knowledge regarding your affairs and should already hold your trust. Of course, you do need to ensure they are up to the task. You should, for example, consider whether they have adequate financial management skills and sufficient time to handle your affairs properly. You should also consider whether they will be able to objectively make decisions on your behalf, keep accurate financial records and preserve the value of your estate.

Ultimately, your agent must be able for the role and the role depends on what you have in mind for them, and the complexity of the task ahead. So, choose wisely and remember your agent can take legal, financial, or other advice. So, they will not be alone in the task.

What Laws Govern My Power of Attorney?

Most powers of attorney contain a 'jurisdiction' clause which sets out the laws which will govern the operation of a power of attorney and, in turn, the agent's authority under it. In many cases, this will be the law of the state in which the principal is resident, and in which the agent is expected to act.

If your agent is expected to act in relation to an asset, such as real estate, located in a different state to where you reside, it can be helpful to make an additional power of attorney which applies to actions taken in that state and which is governed by the laws of that state. This will generally make it easier for your agent's authority under the power of attorney to be accepted by persons wishing to rely on that authority. In some cases, depending on what actions your agent may need to take, it may even make sense to appoint an agent who is resident in that other state. For example, if your agent is expected to manage a real estate project in New York, it may be useful to appoint an agent in New York to do that.

The laws of most states set out what is legally required for a document to be deemed to be a power of attorney. Some states have even issued sample power of attorney forms for use. However, using them is generally not mandatory. For this reason, lawyers frequently prepare powers of attorney for their clients using their own standard terminology rather than adopting state approved forms. As long as the document is headed 'power of attorney', specifies the parties, is signed and dated, and contains recognizable terms normally found in a power of attorney, it should be accepted by most authorities and organizations.

In addition to law firms, banks and brokerage houses also typically have their own power of attorney forms. If you want to ensure that your agent can transact business on your behalf with these institutions, you should consider preparing two (or more) powers of attorney — one being your own form and the others being those required by the institutions with which you propose to do business through your agent. You should check with the relevant institutions in advance to ascertain their specific requirements in relation to power of attorney forms, and even obtain copies of the forms they prefer to use. That way, you can fill in and sign their form at the same time as you prepare and execute your 'general purpose' power of attorney.

If your power of attorney is to be used in a foreign country, you may need to have it 'authenticated' or 'legalized' before it can lawfully be used. This is a process whereby a government official certifies that the authority (usually a notary or lawyer) who is stated on your power of attorney document as having witnessed your sign it is authentic, and can therefore be accepted in the foreign country. For more information about document authentication and legalization, contact the local consulate or embassy of the foreign country in which you propose your power of attorney be used.

In terms of signing and witnessing, different jurisdictions tend to have different requirements for powers of attorney. As such, it's beneficial to double check with the laws applicable in your state to see how your power of attorney should be executed. However, in almost all cases, executing your power of attorney in front of a witness and/or a notary will suffice. We have provided further guidance on the execution process later in this kit.

Witness to a Power of Attorney

To satisfy various jurisdictional requirements, it is advisable that you not use any of the following people as your witnesses:

- your spouse.
- your partner.
- your child.
- your agent or alternate agent.
- the spouse of your agent or alternate agent.
- employees of a medical facility in which you are or may become a patient.

Your witnesses must have reached the age of majority in your state and be of sound mind.

Commencement of a Power of Attorney

The agent's authority under a power of attorney will commence on the date specified in the document or upon the occurrence of a specified event. That event could be the happening of something specific such as the opening of a bank account with a particular bank, or the purchase of a specific piece of real estate; or it could be on the occurrence of your incapacity. You are free to choose the specific date or event.

If no date or event is specified in the power of attorney, then the agent's authority takes immediate effect once the document is validly executed and the agent notified.

Filing or Recording a Power of Attorney

Normally, powers of attorney do not need to be registered with any state body to become legally effective. However, if your agent is going to be acting in relation to a transaction involving land or real estate then the power of attorney will normally need to be registered with the County Clerk, Registry of Deeds or the Land Titles Office (the exact name of filing authority varies from state to state). Absent doing that, your agent's authority to deal with the real estate is not likely to be accepted. Not every state requires registration, so it is sensible to double check the requirements in your state. Where registration is required, the power of attorney document usually needs to be notarized before registration.

There are generally no time frames within which you need to register the power of attorney. It just needs to be registered before your agent seeks to exercise authority under it. If the agent does not need immediate authority to act, and you don't want the document placed on the public record straight away, you can hold off on registering it until it's needed. When the time comes, you or your agent can then register it. However, if you are adopting this approach, you should check with the clerk in the relevant registry of titles to see what the specific requirements for registration are. For example, in some states, power of attorney documents must be a specific size or be on a specific type of paper. If your document meets those requirements, then you can then choose to wait before registering. If not, you need to quickly rectify the problem, or your agent may not be able to act in relation to that real estate.

If you intend to register your power of attorney in the Registry of Deeds in Illinois, Indiana, Kentucky or Minnesota you will also need to complete the "Preparation Statement" section at the end of the power of attorney document in this kit. This section simply identifies the person who has prepared the document. In most cases, this will be you (the principal). However, if someone has prepared it on your behalf, they should be identified in this section.

Revocation of a Power of Attorney

Assuming you are not incapacitated, you can revoke your power of attorney at any time by sending a 'notice of revocation' to your agent. This is a written notice signed by or on behalf of a person who granted a power of attorney stating that he or she is terminating the authority conferred on the agent under a power of attorney.

There are several reasons why you might want to revoke your power of attorney. It may be that:

- your power of attorney is no longer necessary as you can now act on your own behalf.
- you no longer trust your agent.
- you have found a more suitable person to act as your agent.
- it is no longer practical to have your agent acting on your behalf.
- the purpose behind granting your power of attorney has been fulfilled and you no longer need an agent to act on your behalf.

The revocation of a power of attorney is not effective against an agent or any third party who may rely on it until such time as the notice of the revocation has been received by that person. As such, it is common practice to send a written notice of revocation by recorded delivery to the agent and all third parties who may rely on the power of attorney. This then puts them on notice that the agent's authority has been revoked.

Important Points & Recommendation

While a power of attorney can be an exceptionally handy tool, it is important to remember that it is a serious legal document with far-reaching consequences. Therefore, drawing up and signing a power of attorney is something that you should do with due care and forethought.

If, having regard to your own particular circumstances, you are in any doubt as to the adequacy of the forms accompanying this kit or what they do, or about the scope of your agent's authority under them, we recommend you speak to a lawyer before using them.

Did You Know

For further information on powers of attorney, see our book entitled "Make Your Own Power of Attorney".

Important Notice

This is an important legal document. Before signing this document, you should know these important facts:

- This document gives the person you name as your agent the power to make legal and financial decisions on your behalf. Unless you state otherwise in your document, your agent will have the same authority to make legal and financial decisions on your behalf as you would have.

- Your agent's authority to act on your behalf is subject to any limitations you expressly include in your pow¬er of attorney document. Your agent will be obligated to follow your instructions when acting on your behalf.

- After you have signed this document, you will still have the right and authority to make legal and financial decisions for yourself if you are mentally competent to do so.

- You can revoke your power of attorney by written notice to your agent and to any relevant third parties who may rely on the power of attorney - if you are mentally competent to serve such notice.

- As this is not a durable power of attorney, it will automatically terminate if you become incapacitated.

- If there is anything in the documents contained in this kit that you do not understand, you should ask a lawyer, or other suitably qualified person to explain it to you.

Appendices

Appendix 1

Signing Instructions

Instructions for Completing the General Power of Attorney

1. Carefully read all the instructions below.

2. Print out the document and complete it neatly using a pen or carefully edit the text version of the form (that is available to you to downlad) on your computer.

3. On the cover page of the document, insert the date of execution of the power of attorney as well as your name, as principal, in the spaces provided.

4. Clause 1 identifies the parties to the power of attorney. In this clause, you will need to enter (i) your name and address, (ii) that of your primary agent and (iii) that of your alternate agent in the spaces provided.

5. In clause 12, enter your state of residence.

6. If you wish to use a notary, arrange to meet with a notary. Once you meet the notary, you should proceed to step 7 – in the notary's presence. If you do not wish to use a notary, then simply go to step 7 and disregard references to the notary.

7. In the execution block, immediately after clause 12, enter the date, month, year, and place of execution. Then sign your name on the signature line above the words "The Principal" in the presence of the notary and two witnesses.

   Your witnesses should not be a person who is:

   - your agent or attorney-in-fact.
   - the notary acknowledging your signature.
   - a relation by blood, marriage, or adoption to you or your agent; or a spouse of any such person.
   - financially responsible for your medical care.
   - entitled to any portion of your estate following your death.
   - a beneficiary under an insurance policy on your life.
   - entitled to make claim against your estate (such as creditors).
   - your attending physician, nor an employee of such a physician.

8. You should have the two witnesses who witnessed your execution of the power of attorney complete the "Witness Affidavit" section of the document.

9. You should then have a notary complete the "Notary Affidavit" section of the document.

10. If you intend to register your document in the Registry of Deeds in Illinois, Indiana, Kentucky, or Minnesota you will need to complete the "Preparation Statement" section of the document. This section simply identifies the person who has prepared the document. In most cases, this will be you (the principal). However, if someone has prepared it on your behalf, they should be identified in this section.

11. If you live in California, Georgia, Montana, New Hampshire, Pennsylvania, Vermont, or Wisconsin you will need to have your agent accept his or her appointment under the power of attorney before they can lawfully act. You can do this by having your agent complete and sign the Acknowledgement of Agent section of the document.

    In fact, while there is no obligation to do so, it is both recommended and good practice to always get your agent to sign this acknowledgement irrespective of what state you reside it.

12. If your power of attorney is to grant authority over real property to your agent, it should also be registered in the registry of deeds your agent may not be deemed to have authority to deal with your real property.

    When you register the document is largely up to you as there are generally no time requirements for registration. If it is not needed straight away, and you do not want the document placed on public record straight away, you can hold off on registering it until it is needed. When the time comes, your agent can then register it. However, if you are adopting this approach, you need to check with the clerk in the registry of deeds to see what the specific requirements are for registering. For example, in some states, the documents must be a specific size or on specific types of paper. If your document meets the required standards, you can then choose to wait before registering.

Instructions for Completing the Agent's Acceptance of Appointment

1. Carefully read all the instructions below.

2. Print out the document and complete it neatly using a pen or carefully edit the text version of the form (that is available to you to download) on your computer.

3. The first paragraph identifies the agent and the principal. Therefore, in this paragraph, you will need to enter (i) the name of your agent and (ii) that of the principal in the spaces provided. Your agent will then need to date and sign the document at the bottom of the page, as well as specify his address.

4. If the power of attorney document grants the agent authority to deal with real estate, the agent should sign the document in front of a notary.

Instructions for Completing the Notice of Revocation of a Power of Attorney

1. Carefully read all the instructions below.

2. Print out the document and complete it neatly using a pen or carefully edit the text version of the form (that is available to you to download) on your computer.

3. On the cover page of the document, insert the date of execution of the notice of revocation as well as your name, as principal, in the spaces provided.

4. The first paragraph of the document identifies the parties to the original power of attorney and its date. In this paragraph, you will need to enter (i) your name and address, (ii) the date of the power of attorney and (iii) the name of your agent.

5. Arrange to meet with a notary if you wish to use a notary. Once you meet the notary, you should proceed to step 6 – in the notary's presence. If you do not wish to use a notary, then simply go to step 6 and disregard references to the notary.

6. In the execution block, enter the date, month, year, and place of execution. Then sign your name on the signature line above the words "The Principal" in the presence of the notary and two witnesses.

    Your witnesses should not be a person who is:

    *   your agent or attorney-in-fact.

    *   the notary acknowledging your signature.

    *   a relation by blood, marriage, or adoption to you or your agent; or a spouse of any such person.

    *   financially responsible for your medical care.

    *   entitled to any portion of your estate following your death.

    *   a beneficiary under an insurance policy on your life.

    *   entitled to make claim against your estate (such as creditors).

    *   your attending physician, nor an employee of such a physician.

7. You should have the two witnesses who witnessed your execution of the notice of revocation complete the "Witness Affidavit" section of the document.

8. You should then have a notary complete the "Notary Affidavit" section of the document.

Appendix 2

General Power of Attorney For Finance and Property

Downloadable Forms

Blank copies of all this form can be downloaded from the EstateBee website. Simply login to your account or, if you don't have an account, you can create one for free.

www.estate-bee.com/login

Once logged in, go to your profile page and enter the code listed below in the 'Use Codes' tab:

GenPOA553A

Dated this _____ day of _____, 20____

_____

General Power of Attorney

of

_____

(Principal)

> **Notice:** The powers granted by this document are broad and sweeping. If you have any questions about these powers, obtain competent legal advice. This document does not authorize anyone to make medical and other healthcare decisions for you. You may revoke this power of attorney if you later wish to do so provided you are of sound mind.

EstateBee

www.estate-bee.com

General Power of Attorney

1. I, _____ of _____ aged eighteen years and upwards hereby appoint _____ of _____ _ as my lawfully appointed attorney in fact (referred to as my "Agent") on and subject to the terms and conditions set out below. If for any reason this person shall be unable or unwilling to act as my Agent, I hereby appoint _____ of _____ _____ to act as my Agent instead subject to the terms and conditions set out herein.

2. This power of attorney shall apply for financial and property applications only and shall remain effective until my incapacity, death, or until revoked by me in writing.

3. This power of attorney shall become and is hereby effective immediately and will continue in full force and effect until terminated in accordance with the provisions of Clause 2. This power of attorney shall, for the avoidance of doubt, be construed as a general power of attorney.

4. I hereby grant (subject to the provisions of Clause 6) my Agent full power and authority over all my finances and property, both real and personal, and authorize my Agent to do and perform each and every act which I could do or perform and I hereby ratify and confirm all that my Agent shall do or cause to be done under this Power of Attorney.

5. Without prejudice to the provisions of Clause 4 but subject always to the provisions of Clause 6, my Agent's powers shall include, but shall not be limited to, the power to:

    (a) **Real property transactions**

    receive from any person, to retain and to invest and reinvest in any kind of property or investment; to dispose of any property or any interest therein at such times and upon such terms and conditions as shall seem proper and to give good and sufficient instruments of transfer and to receive the proceeds of any such disposition; to purchase, manage, maintain and insure any property and to lease the same for such periods and on such terms as shall seem advantageous, and if advisable to pay for the value of any improvements made by a tenant under any such lease; to incur, extend or renew mortgage indebtedness; to make ordinary and extraordinary repairs and alterations to any building, to raze or erect buildings and to make improvements or to abandon any buildings or property; and to make any agreement of partition of such property and to give or receive money or other property in connection therewith;

    (b) **Personal property transactions**

    buy, sell, mortgage, hypothecate, assign, transfer, grant options over and deal with all my personal property, tangible or intangible; and to manage, improve, repair and lease same; and to make, do, and transact all and every kind of business of whatever nature in respect thereto; and in each case in such manner and on such terms as my agent deems proper;

(c) **Commercial transactions**

manage, sell, administer, liquidate, continue, discontinue or otherwise deal with any corporation, partnership or other business interest of mine as my Agent deems fit; to engage, compensate and discharge employees, agents, professional advisors and consultants; to assent to, oppose and participate in any reorganization, recapitalization, merger, consolidation or similar proceeding, to deposit securities, delegate discretionary powers, pay assessments or other expenses and exchange property, all as fully as might be done by persons owning similar property in their own right;

(d) **Financial transactions**

open, administer, manage and close bank, savings, loans brokerage, and other such accounts in my name, to lodge proceeds to and withdraw proceeds from such accounts, to receive, draw, endorse and sign checks, bank drafts, bills of exchange, loan notes, promissory notes, letters of credit and certificates of deposit in relation to any such account and the proceeds therein; to pay any sums owing in respect of any such account, to use all credit cards issued in my name; to borrow such sums of money as my Agent may from time to time deem fit and to secure any such obligations by mortgage or pledge and to execute all documents in connection therewith;

(e) **Financial securities**

purchase, exercise, surrender, transfer, sell or otherwise dispose of all rights, options, powers and privileges, and to vote in person or by proxy, in relation to any stocks, bonds or other securities, all as fully as might be done by persons owning similar property in their own right;

(f) **Commodity and option transactions**

buy, sell, transfer and deal in commodities and options of all types; and to exercise all powers and do all matters and things incidental to the same;

(g) **Insurance and annuity transactions**

exercise or perform any act or do any thing in connection with any insurance cover I may have in my name (including, but not limited to, taking out new cover, paying premiums, making claims, extending cover, renewing polices and terminating policies) which my Agent deems necessary or prudent to maintain the value of my real or personal property;

(h) **Estate and trust transactions**

demand, sue for, collect, and receive all legacies, bequests, and gifts due, payable or belonging to me, and take all lawful means, for the recovery thereof and to compromise the same and give discharges for the same; and to transfer any interest I may have in property, whether real or personal, tangible or intangible, to the trustee of any trust that I have created for my benefit;

(i) **Retirement plans**

create and contribute to any type of retirement plan established in my name or for my benefit; to select any payment option under any retirement plan in which I am a participant or change options I have selected; to make voluntary contributions to such plans; to "roll-over" plan benefits into other retirement plans; to borrow money and purchase assets therefrom and sell assets thereto, if authorized by any such plan; to receive benefits from and engage in transactions (including the making of any plan election) with any retirement plan of which I am a beneficiary, and to exercise all powers necessary or desirable in connection with the maintenance and administration of such plans;

(j) **Family maintenance**

do all things and acts to maintain and support my family, including the making of any payments to and on behalf of my family that my Agent reasonably deems fit; and to hire accountants, attorneys at law, consultants, clerks, physicians, nurses, agents, servants, workmen, and others and to remove them, and to appoint others in their place, and to pay and allow the persons so employed such salaries, wages, or other remunerations, as my Agent shall deem proper;

(k) **Benefits**

prepare, execute and file any application or claim for any government, insurance, medical, military or social security benefit that I may be entitled to receive, to receive personal, confidential and medical information; to settle, compromise or contest any related assessments made against me; and to represent me in all matters relating to same;

(l) **Claims and litigation**

initiate, discontinue, defend and settle all actions, demands, claims and legal proceedings, by arbitration or otherwise, in connection with any or all of my real and personal property and any rights, interests or entitlements that I may have or any matters in which I am in any way concerned, in such manner as my Agent shall deem fit; and to give appropriate discharges, releases and receipt for the same;

(m) **Taxation**

prepare, execute and file any and all tax and informational returns that I may be entitled or required to make; to pay any taxes, surcharges and penalties duly owing by me, to file claims for tax refunds of every description; to settle, compromise or contest any tax assessments made against me; and to represent me in all matters before the Internal Revenue Service;

(n) **Safe deposit box**

access any safety deposit box registered in my name alone or jointly with others, and to remove any property or papers located therein; and

(o) **Deal with contracts**

enter into, negotiate, alter, amend, revoke, and exercise all rights granted under contracts of all types.

6. My Agent shall have no authority to give any of my property to, or to use any of my property for the benefit of, himself or herself. In addition, my agent (i) cannot execute a will, a codicil, or any will substitute on my behalf; (ii) cannot change the beneficiary on any life insurance policy that I own; (iii) cannot make gifts on my behalf; (iv) may not exercise any powers that would cause any assets of mine to be considered taxable to my agent or to my agent's estate for purposes of any income, estate, or inheritance tax, and (v) cannot contravene any medical or healthcare power of attorney or living will I have executed whether prior or subsequent to the execution of this Power of Attorney.

7. The powers conferred on my Agent herein may be exercised by my Agent alone, and my Agent's signature or act under the authority granted herein may be accepted by any third person or organization as fully authorized by me and with the same legal force and effect as if I were personally present, competent and acting on my own behalf.

8. Third parties may rely upon the representations of the Agent as to all matters regarding powers granted to the Agent. No person who acts in reliance on the authority granted under this Power of Attorney shall incur any liability to me or to my estate for permitting the Agent to exercise any power prior to actual knowledge that the Power of Attorney has been revoked or terminated by operation of law or otherwise.

9. No agent named or substituted in this Power of Attorney shall incur any liability to me for acting or refraining from acting under this power, except for such agent's own misconduct, fraud or negligence.

10. My Agent shall provide an accounting for all funds and assets handled and all acts performed as my Agent, if I so request or if such a request is made by any authorized personal representative or fiduciary properly acting on my behalf. My Agent shall not however be obliged to file any such accountings or any inventory with a court and any obligation in this respect is hereby waived to the fullest extent permitted by law.

11. My Agent shall be reimbursed for reasonable expenses incurred while acting as my Agent and may receive reasonable compensation for acting as Agent.

12. This power of attorney will be governed by the laws of the State of _____ without regard for conflicts of laws principles and is intended to be valid in all jurisdictions of the United States of America and all foreign nations.

Executed this _____ day of _____, 20_____, at

_____

_____

_____

The Principal

Witness Affidavit

I declare, on the basis of information and belief, that the person who signed or acknowledged this document (the principal) is personally known to me, that he/she signed or acknowledged this Power of Attorney in my presence, and that he/she appears to be of sound mind and under no duress, fraud, or undue influence. I am not related to the principal by blood, marriage, or adoption, either as a spouse, a lineal ancestor, descendant of the parents of the principal, or spouse of any of them. I am not directly financially responsible for the principal's medical care. I am not entitled to any portion of the principal's estate upon his/her decease, whether under any Will or as an heir by intestate succession, nor am I the beneficiary of an insurance policy on the principal's life, nor do I have a claim against the principal's estate as of this time. I am not the principal's attending physician, nor an employee of the attending physician. No more than one witness is an employee of a health facility in which the principal is a patient. I am not appointed as Healthcare Agent or Successor Healthcare Agent by this document.

Witness No. 1

Signature: _____

Date: _____

Print Name: _____

Telephone: _____

Residence Address: _____

_____

_____

_____

Witness No. 2

Signature: _____

Date: _____

Print Name: _____

Telephone: _____

Residence Address: _____

_____

_____

_____

Notary Affidavit

State of _____   County of _____

On _____ before me, _____, a notary public, personally appeared _____, who proved to me on the basis of satisfactory evidence to be the person whose name is subscribed to the within instrument and acknowledged to me that he/she executed the same in his/her authorized capacity, and that by his/her signature on the instrument he/she executed the instrument. I certify under PENALTY OF PERJURY that the foregoing is true and correct. Witness my hand and official seal.

Signature: _____

Print Name: _____

My commission expires on: _____

(Seal)

Preparation Statement

This document was prepared by the following individual:

_____

Print Name

_____

Signature

Acknowledgment of Agent

By accepting or acting under the appointment, the agent assumes the fiduciary and other legal responsibilities of an agent.

_____

Print Name of Agent

_____

Signature of Agent

Appendix 3

Agent's Acceptance of Appointment
(For Use in Georgia Only)

Downloadable Forms

Blank copies of all this form can be downloaded from the EstateBee website. Simply login to your account or, if you don't have an account, you can create one for free.

www.estate-bee.com/login

Once logged in, go to your profile page and enter the code listed below in the 'Use Codes' tab:

GenPOA553A

Acceptance of Appointment

I, _____ (print name), have read the foregoing Power of Attorney and am the person identified therein as Agent for _____ (name of grantor of power of attorney), the Principal named therein. I hereby acknowledge the following:

(i)   I owe a duty of loyalty and good faith to the Principal and must use the powers granted to me only for the benefit of the Principal.

(ii)   I must keep the Principal's funds and other assets separate and apart from my funds and other assets and titled in the name of the Principal. I must not transfer title to any of the Principal's funds or other assets into my name alone. My name must not be added to the title of any funds or other assets of the Principal, unless I am specifically designated as Agent for the Principal in the title.

(iii)   I must protect, conserve, and exercise prudence and caution in my dealings with the Principal's funds and other assets.

(iv)   I must keep a full and accurate record of my acts, receipts, and disbursements on behalf of the Principal, and be ready to account to the Principal for such acts, receipts, and disbursements at all times. I must provide an annual accounting to the Principal of my acts, receipts, and disbursements, and must furnish an accounting of such acts, receipts, and disbursements to the personal representative of the Principal's estate within 90 days after the date of death of the Principal.

I have read the Compensation of Agent paragraph in the Power of Attorney and agree to abide by it.

I acknowledge my authority to act on behalf of the Principal ceases at the death of the Principal.

I hereby accept the foregoing appointment as Agent for the Principal with full knowledge of the responsibilities imposed on me, and I will faithfully carry out my duties to the best of my ability.

Dated:_____, _____.

(Signature)_____

(Address)_____

Note: A notarized signature is not required unless the Principal has included instructions regarding property transactions.

I, _____, a Notary Public, do hereby certify that _____
_____ personally appeared before me this date and acknowledged the due execution of the foregoing Acceptance of Appointment.

_____

Notary Public

Appendix 4

Notice of Revocation of a Power of Attorney

Downloadable Forms

Blank copies of all this form can be downloaded from the EstateBee website. Simply login to your account or, if you don't have an account, you can create one for free.

www.estate-bee.com/login

Once logged in, go to your profile page and enter the code listed below in the 'Use Codes' tab:

Revocation553A

Dated this _____ day of _____, 20 __

_____

Notice of Revocation

of

_____

(Principal)

_____

Estate *Bee*

www.estate-bee.com

Notice of Revocation

I, _____ of _____ aged
eighteen years and upwards hereby revoke, countermand and make null and void the Power of
Attorney dated _____ (the "Power of Attorney") and granted in favor of __
_____ (the "Agent", which expression shall include any successor
agent appointed under the Power of Attorney) and all rights, powers and authority thereby given
to the Agent shall hereby lapse and cease.

Executed this _____ day of _____, 20 _____, at _____
_____.

_____
The Principal

Witness Affidavit

I declare, on the basis of information and belief, that the person who signed or acknowledged
this document (the principal) is personally known to me, that he/she signed or acknowledged
this Notice of Revocation of a Power of Attorney in my presence, and that he/she appears to be
of sound mind and under no duress, fraud, or undue influence. I am not related to the principal
by blood, marriage, or adoption, either as a spouse, a lineal ancestor, descendant of the parents of
the principal, or spouse of any of them. I am not directly financially responsible for the principal's
medical care. I am not entitled to any portion of the principal's estate upon his/her decease,
whether under any Will or as an heir by intestate succession, nor am I the beneficiary of an
insurance policy on the principal's life, nor do I have a claim against the principal's estate as of this
time. I am not the principal's attending physician, nor an employee of the attending physician. No
more than one witness is an employee of a health facility in which the principal is a patient. I am
not appointed as Healthcare Agent or Successor Healthcare Agent by this document.

Witness No. 1

Signature: _____

Date: _____

Print Name: _____

Telephone: _____

Residence Address: _____

_____

_____

_____

Witness No. 2

Signature: _____

Date: _____

Print Name: _____

Telephone: _____

Residence Address: _____

_____

_____

_____

Notary Affidavit

State of _____   County of _____

On _____ before me, _____, a notary public, personally appeared _____, who proved to me on the basis of satisfactory evidence to be the person whose name is subscribed to the within instrument and acknowledged to me that he/she executed the same in his/her authorized capacity, and that by his/her signature on the instrument he/she executed the instrument. I certify under PENALTY OF PERJURY that the foregoing is true and correct. Witness my hand and official seal.

Signature: _____

Print Name: _____

My commission expires on: _____

(Seal)

EstateBee's Estate Planning Range

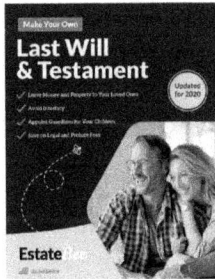

Make Your Own Last Will & Testament

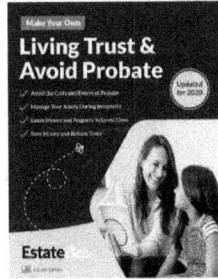

Make Your Own Living Trust & Avoid Probate

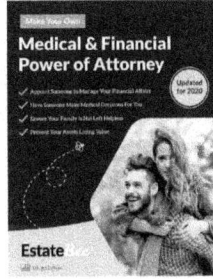

Make Your Own Medical & Financial Power of Attorney

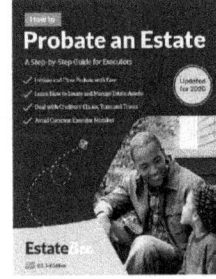

How to Probate an Estate - A Step-by-Step Guide for Executors

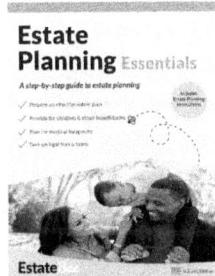

Estate Planning Essentials - A Step-by-Step Guide to Estate Planning

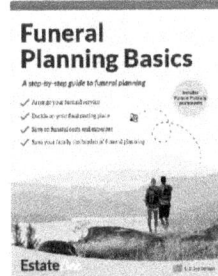

Funeral Planning Basics – A Step-by-Step Guide to Funeral Planning

Legal Will Kit

Living Trust Kit

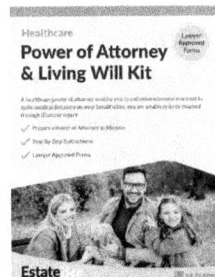

Healthcare Power of Attorney & Living Will Kit

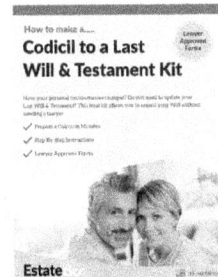

Codicil to a Last Will & Testament Kit

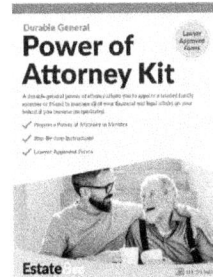

Durable General Power of Attorney Kit

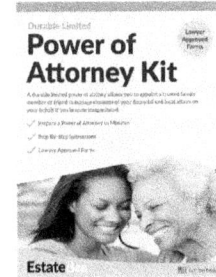

Durable Limited Power of Attorney Kit

www.ingramcontent.com/pod-product-compliance
Lightning Source LLC
Chambersburg PA
CBHW051233200326
41519CB00025B/7363